KT-441-732

MEASURE IT!

MASS AND WEIGHT

Barbara A. Somervill

C555047508

www.raintreepublishers.co.uk
Visit our website to find out more information about Raintree books.

To order:
☎ Phone 0845 6044371
🖨 Fax +44 (0) 1865 312263
🖳 Email myorders@raintreepublishers.co.uk

Customers from outside the UK please telephone +44 1865 312262

Raintree is an imprint of Capstone Global Library Limited, a company incorporated in England and Wales having its registered office at 7 Pilgrim Street, London, EC4V 6LB – Registered company number: 6695582

Text © Capstone Global Library Limited
First published in hardback in 2010
Published in paperback in 2011
The moral rights of the proprietor have been asserted.

All rights reserved. No part of this publication may be reproduced in any form or by any means (including photocopying or storing it in any medium by electronic means and whether or not transiently or incidentally to some other use of this publication) without the written permission of the copyright owner, except in accordance with the provisions of the Copyright, Designs and Patents Act 1988 or under the terms of a licence issued by the Copyright Licensing Agency, Saffron House, 6–10 Kirby Street, London EC1N 8TS (www.cla.co.uk). Applications for the copyright owner's written permission should be addressed to the publisher.

Edited by Megan Cotugno, Louise Galpine, and Abby Colich
Designed by Richard Parker
Original illustrations © Capstone Global Library Ltd (2010)
Illustrated by Darren Lingard
Picture research by Mica Brancic
Originated by Capstone Global Library Ltd
Printed in China by CTPS

ISBN 978 0 431085 18 0 (hardback)
14 13 12 11 10
10 9 8 7 6 5 4 3 2 1

ISBN 978 0 431085 24 1 (paperback)
15 14 13 12 11
10 9 8 7 6 5 4 3 2 1

British Library Cataloguing in Publication Data
Somervill, Barbara A.
Mass and weight. – (Measure it!)
A full catalogue record for this book is available from the British Library.

Acknowledgements
We would like to thank the following for permission to reproduce photographs: Corbis p. 27; Getty Images pp. 19 (©Francesco Bittichesu), 24 (©StockTrek); iStockphoto pp. 4 (©nullplus), 10 (©web photographer) 12 (©kutay tanir), 15 (©Elemental Imaging), 18 (©mikadx) 21 (©Chris Fourie), 22 (©Henry Chaplin), 25 (Getty Images/Hulton Archive); NASA pp. 8 (Johnson Space Center), 28; Photolibrary p. 6 (Imagestate/©Piers Cavendish); Science Photo Library p. 14 (© Charles D. Winters); Shutterstock pp. 11 (© Seleznev Valery), 13 (© Baldovina), 16 (© Francois Etienne du Plessis).

Cover photo of dial on weight scale reproduced with permission from Photolibrary (Thomas Northcut).

We would like to thank John Pucek for his invaluable help in the preparation of this book.

Every effort has been made to contact copyright holders of material reproduced in this book. Any omissions will be rectified in subsequent printings if notice is given to the publishers.

Disclaimer
All the Internet addresses (URLs) given in this book were valid at the time of going to press. However, due to the dynamic nature of the Internet, some addresses may have changed, or sites may have changed or ceased to exist since publication. While the author and publisher regret any inconvenience this may cause readers, no responsibility for any such changes can be accepted by either the author or the publisher.

Contents

Some words are printed in bold, **like this**. You can find out what they mean by looking in the glossary on page 30.

What is mass?

Mass is easy to define but difficult to understand. Mass is how much matter or "stuff" there is in something. This book is made up of matter and has mass. Its mass comes from the paper, ink, and glue that make up the book.

You may have heard of mass talked about as bulk or size. In science, mass does not mean large, although large objects have mass. A building, a whale, and a planet are large objects that have mass. Very small objects also have mass. A single **atom**, a grain of sand, and a feather all have mass.

Something as small and light as a feather still has mass.

Let's look at mass and the human body. Your body has mass. Your bones, muscles, blood, and other body parts contain atoms. When you receive a haircut, the loss of hair reduces your mass. When you eat breakfast, your mass becomes greater. You have added more matter to your body. Although these changes are very small, they are changes in mass. Even pulling out a single strand of hair or eating a peanut changes the mass of a person's body.

Balancing mass

Mass matters when trying to balance two objects. Two children go to a playground and ride on a see-saw. The children have similar masses and can make the see-saw work as designed. As one pushes up, the other goes down. The **force** needed to push one end up is not so great, because the mass on the other end of the see-saw helps pull that end down. A third child climbs on one end of the see-saw. The mass on one end is now much greater than on the other end. The mass is not evenly balanced, and it is hard to make the see-saw work.

Work it out

Luke, Abby, Emma, and Jamie want to ride on a see-saw. The table below shows the mass of each child. How should the children pair up so that the see-saw comes close to balancing?

Name	Mass in kilograms (kg)
Luke	39
Abby	24
Emma	37
Jamie	23

Mass, force, and motion

Another way we use mass in everyday life is with motion. A force acts on an object and causes it to move. A force is simply a push or pull. The larger the mass of the object, the greater the force needed to move it.

Look at the photo of the full train below. An empty train contains less matter than a full train. A train engine has to move the total mass of the train. This includes the engine, train, people, luggage, food, drinks, and all other objects on the train. **Engineers** need to know about mass when they design vehicles such as jets, trains, cars, and motorcycles.

Engineers need to know the total mass of a train to design brakes that will stop the train.

What is gravity?

Gravity is a universal force that acts between all objects. All objects feel the force of gravity. On Earth it is gravity that causes objects to pick up speed as they fall. This is because the gravitational force between Earth and the objects **accelerates** the object. The amount of gravitational force that each object experiences depends on that object's mass.

Mass and weight

Scientists and engineers use mass to work out other properties of objects, such as **weight** or **density**. Mass should not be confused with weight. Weight is a measure of the downward pull of gravity on an object. An astronaut's mass on Earth does not change when he goes into space. If his mass is 85 kilograms on Earth, it is also 85 kilograms in space, on the moon, or on Mars. But if that astronaut goes to Mars, his weight will be different because the force of gravity is different on Mars.

Mass and density

Density also depends on mass. Density compares the mass of two objects of the same size. To find density, divide the mass of the object by the **volume**. You will learn more about density and how to measure density on page 24.

> **Did you know?**
> The terms "mass" and "weight" are often thought of as the same thing, but they are actually very different. Weight is a measure of the downward pull of gravity on an object. Mass is a measure of how much matter an object has. When someone asks how much you weigh, they are actually talking about your mass.

Although this astronaut is floating in space, his mass has not changed.

What units are used when measuring mass?

Mass is most commonly measured in metric units. The gram is the base unit of **mass**. The mass of very small objects, such as the amount of sodium in a tin of soup, is measured in milligrams. The mass of slightly larger objects, such as an apple, is measured in grams. The mass of a car is measured in **kilograms**.

Units of mass

Unit of mass	Unit equivalent
milligram (mg)	1/1,000 of a gram
gram (g)	1 gram
kilogram (kg)	1,000 grams

Mass is most commonly measured in metric units.

Which has the greater mass – a pencil or a pen? Does either one have more mass than a granola bar or an egg? You can look at an object and guess its mass. You can compare the mass of one object against another object using a **balance**. The most precise way to know the mass of an object is to use a balance or scale. For small objects, a triple-beam balance gives the most accurate measure.

Did you know?
The **standard** for the kilogram is a block of platinum and iridium held in a vault in Sèvres, France. It has been the standard since 1889. All accurate metric mass measurements are based on the Sèvres standard.

What are scales and balances?

The tools used for measuring both **mass** and **weight** are scales and **balances**. Balances have been used for about 6,000 years. They compare the mass or weight of multiple objects. The basic parts of a balance are a **fulcrum**, a beam, and two pans that hang from each end of the beam. When both pans are empty, they hang level or balanced. Place an object on one pan, and the pan will drop down. Place an object of equal mass or weight on the second pan, and the two pans become level again.

With a balance, you can tell if two items are of equal mass even if you don't know what that mass is.

Here's an example of how you might use a balance: Someone wishes to trade you an equal weight of fish for wheat. The fish is put on one pan of a double-pan balance. A sack of wheat is placed on the other pan. Wheat is added or taken away until both pans balance. Balances can also be used with **standard** weights. Balances are still used in many markets around the world.

Standard weights

Before weight standards were made, people used common food products on their balances. In India mustard seed was used for balancing the weight of gold dust. Wheat and barley have also been used as weight standards for balances. Balances are ideal for measuring medicine, herbs, spices, gold dust, and precious gems, all of which are small items.

This photo shows standard weights that are used to weigh objects on a double-pan balance.

Scales

Scales come in a wide variety of sizes, shapes, and uses. One difference between a scale and a balance is that a scale shows the amount of mass or weight being measured. Some people might have a scale in their bathrooms. Step on a scale and it gives you an actual number in kilograms or pounds.

A scale, like this bathroom scale to the left, shows the actual amount of mass or weight an object or person has.

This is a spring scale. Objects are placed in the pan, and the weight of the objects pull down on the spring and cause the dial **indicator** to move.

Some bathroom scales are spring scales. Most scales in supermarkets, kitchens, butchers' shops, and sweet shops are spring scales. All scales have specific ranges of numbers depending on what they are being used for. Large scales weigh lorries, orders for gravel or stone, or elephants. Smaller scales weigh human beings. You cannot weigh an elephant and a human on the same scale. Still smaller scales weigh meat, fruit, and vegetables. A kitchen scale can weigh ingredients for a recipe in grams or ounces. Some medical scales can weigh in milligrams.

Triple-beam balance

To use a triple-beam balance, place an object on the pan. Slide the large weight to the right until the beam arm moves close to the zero mark at the right. Lock that weight in place. Next, repeat the process with the topmost weight. Then use the lowest weight. Add the measurements together to find the total mass to the nearest hundredth of a gram.

Use a triple-beam balance to find the most accurate mass of an object.

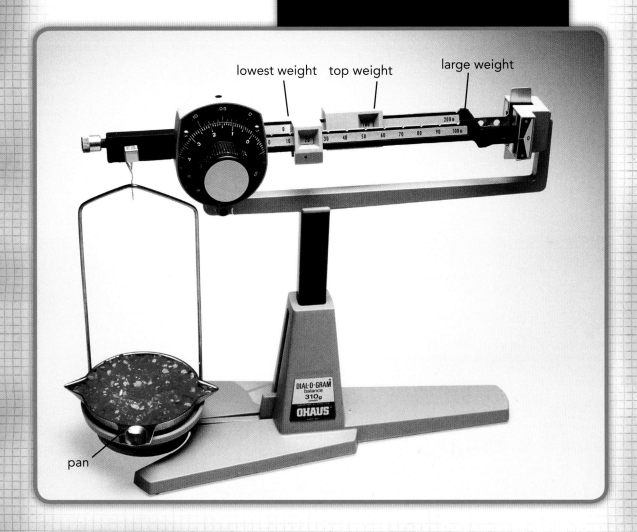

lowest weight   top weight   large weight

pan

Work it out

A scientist places a rock sample on a triple-beam balance. He records the readings from each weight. The readings are 300 grams, 80 grams, and 7.63 grams. What is the total mass of the rock sample?

To make an accurate measure of mass, you need specific tools. An exact measurement of mass is made using scales or balances. It is also possible to **estimate** the mass of an object by comparing it to the mass of another substance. Which has more mass – 10 millilitres of water or 10 millilitres of olive oil? They both have the same **volume**. You get a clue if you pour the olive oil into the water. What happens? The olive oil has less mass. It floats on top of the water.

Scientists use an electric scale to measure the mass of small objects in milligrams or grams.

What is weight?

On the day you were born, one of the first things the hospital did was weigh you. Every time you've been to the doctor since then, you've been weighed again. Doctors compare your **weight** to the average weight of other children your age or to other people your height. Weight is often used to tell if a child is in good health.

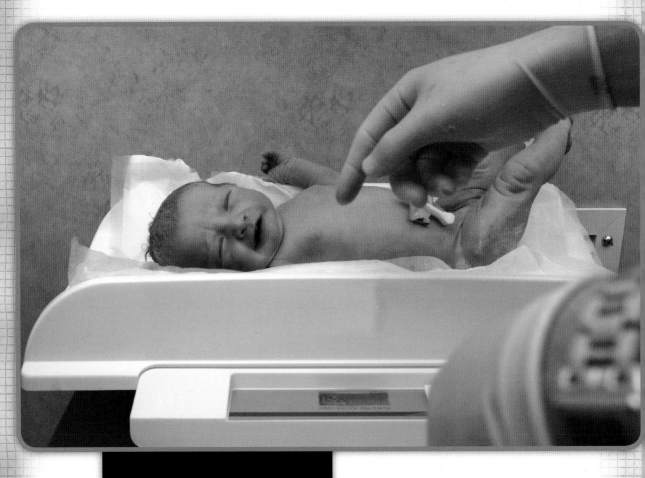

Babies are weighed in grams or pounds and ounces.

Weight and gravity

Earth's force of **gravity** pulls on your body. We measure this effect of gravity as weight. Weight is the measurement of the force of gravity between two objects. A weight scale measures the pulling force – gravity – between two objects. Therefore, your weight is a measurement of the force of gravity between you and Earth.

Measuring weight in the past

For centuries local markets used their own sets of **standard** weights. Not all of the standards were fair weight measures. If a buyer bought barley by weight, that buyer did not know if the seller used honest weights. Traders may not have understood the weight standards used in foreign markets. As trading grew worldwide, the need for a common standard became important.

By the late 1700s, the French were using so many different measurement standards, it caused lots of confusion. In 1790 the French Academy of Science was asked to come up with an easy-to-use measurement system. They developed the metric system. For mass, scientists used the *gram*. The word gram came from the Greek word *gramma*, which means "small weight". The gram became the base unit for all metric weights, which ranged from the small milligram (1/1,000 of a gram) to the **kilogram** (1,000 grams) and the metric ton (1,000 kilograms).

> **Did you know?**
> Where did the pound come from? The weight unit called a pound originally came from the Roman *libra*, meaning "scale". The abbreviation for pound, lb, also comes from this word. At one time, a pound in Britain ranged from 5,400 to 7,680 grains, and each grain was one **barleycorn**. Queen Elizabeth I determined the weight of a pound at 7,000 grains and divided that weight into 16 equal portions, which we call ounces.

Individual wheat grains were once used as a measure of weight. This wheat, however, is shipped by the tonne.

The metric system

Most countries have adopted the metric system. That means that the gram has become the worldwide weight standard, which makes international trade easier. Smaller packaged goods are sold and shipped by grams or kilograms. Bulk products, such as wheat or corn, are weighed, shipped, and sold by the tonne (1,000 kilograms), or the US ton (2,000 pounds).

Weight plays an important role in our everyday lives. As we push our trolleys through a supermarket, we pick up packs of cereal, spices, flour, tea, and dog food. These items are all sold by weight. Weights are printed on the packaging so that we know how much we are buying. We buy hamburger, chicken, and fish by weight, as well as fruits and vegetables.

Airlines weigh luggage to see if suitcases meet the weight requirements.

Work it out

A coffee shop receives a bulk shipment of 50 kilograms of coffee. The shop sells the coffee in bags that weigh 125 grams. How many 125-gram bags can the shop assistants make from the 50-kilogram shipment?

What units are used when measuring weight?

Here we will use the terms **mass** and **weight** interchangeably. This is because on Earth, every object is experiencing the same **force** of **gravity**, and weight really equals the force of gravity acting on an object. Worldwide, metric measurement units are used to measure the weight of objects. Grams and **kilograms** are recognized weight **standards**.

Metric weight (mass) measures

Unit	Metric value	Imperial equivalent
milligram (mg)	1/1,000 gram	0.00004 ounce
gram (g)	1 gram	0.04 ounce
kilogram (kg)	1,000 grams	2.2 pounds
tonne	1,000 kg	2,204 pounds

Sometimes the imperial weight system is used. This system is based on the *avoirdupois* weight system, which originated in Britain. *Avoirdupois* comes from the French for "goods of weight". Common units in the imperial system include the ounce, the pound, and the ton.

Imperial weight (mass) measures

Unit	Imperial value	Metric equivalent
grain	1 grain	65 milligrams
dram	27 grains	1.8 grams
ounce	16 dram or 438 grains	28.3 grams
pound	16 ounces or 7,000 grains	454 grams
hundredweight	100 pounds	45.4 kilograms
ton (long, UK)	2,240 pounds	1,016 kilograms
ton (short, US)	2,000 pounds	907 kilograms

Elephants and cars are generally measured by the tonne.

Large objects and products sold in bulk require larger, heavier weight measures. The unit called a hundredweight refers to one hundred pounds and is used for milk, cheese, and other dairy products. You can also buy grain, seed, flour, sugar, and other food products by the hundredweight. For really heavy weights, such as elephants or cars, weight is measured by the tonne or the ton. A tonne is a metric ton or 1,000 kilograms. Tons come in long and short. A long ton was used in the old British or imperial system and weighed 2,240 pounds. A short ton is used in the US system and weighs 2,000 pounds.

Measuring small objects

Some professions have their own weight system. In jewellery, for example, gold and silver weights are measured in Troy weights. In this system, the smallest unit is the grain. Twenty-four grains equal one pennyweight, and twelve ounces equals one pound Troy. Another weight measure that only jewellers use is the **carat**. Carats measure the weight of diamonds, emeralds, sapphires, and other gems. One carat equals 200 milligrams.

Gems are measured in carats, a weight system only used by jewellers.

In the miniature world of micro sciences, scientists use the very smallest measure of weight, the nanogram. A nanogram weighs one billionth of a gram. Nanograms are used in gene technology. They are also used to measure the amount of toxin or other substances found in food or human blood. Humans cannot measure nanograms – only computers can do that.

Work it out

Look at the scale. How much do the bananas weigh? How much weight is that in grams? (HINT: See the chart on page 20.)

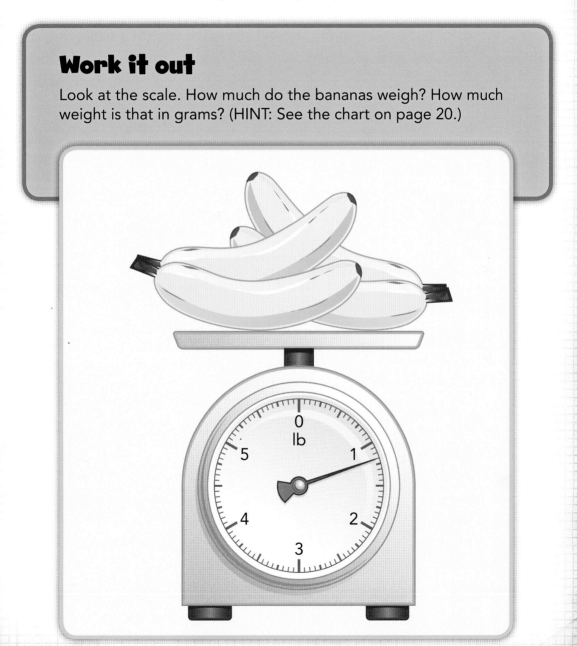

Why do things float?

The reason that some objects float and others sink has to do with **density**. Density compares the **mass** of an object to the **volume** it occupies. The density of a liquid, such as water, depends on the **kilograms** (mass) per litre or pounds per gallon of the water. For solid objects, such as a block of wood, the measure is kilograms per cubic metre or pounds per cubic foot or yard. Objects that have less density than water float. Objects that have more density than water sink.

Put a 10-kilogram block of steel in water, and it will sink. Steel is much denser than water. Yet an aircraft carrier has a mass of many tonnes, and it floats. How can that be?

The design of this ship allows heavier-than-water materials to float.

Did you know?
Greek mathematician Archimedes (287–212 BCE) made a discovery that explains why some things float and others do not. Legend has it that Archimedes made this discovery in his bath! He found that when an object sank into a tub of water, its mass **displaced** an equal mass of water.

According to legend, Archimedes shouted "Eureka!" (Greek for "I found it!") when he realised that his body mass displaced an equal mass of water.

Density

Objects that are full of air have less mass and float well, like a hollow ball. Objects that have little air and more mass have greater density. They sink. You can try this out yourself. Make two clay balls, each with a mass of 100 grams. Reshape one of the balls into a bowl shape. Place the clay ball and the clay bowl in a bucket of water. What happens? By changing the shape of the clay, you added a volume of air and reduced the density.

The distribution of mass allows an aircraft carrier to float. The ship is a huge, heavy mass that is hollow and filled with air. Density is also the reason that hot air balloons float. The volume of hot air in the balloon is less dense and lighter than the cold air outside the balloon. The lighter gas allows the balloon to float in the air.

What is weightlessness?

On Earth our bodies have a weight that is equal to our mass times the **acceleration** of **gravity** at Earth's surface. You might have learned that the acceleration of gravity is equal to 9.8 metres per second squared (m/s^2).

When we are talking about the actual *weight* of an object – in this case a person – we would multiply that person's mass by 9.8 m/s^2. We would then get a number in **Newtons**. A girl with 40 kilograms of mass would weigh 392 Newtons on Earth (40 kilograms x 9.8 m/s^2). If that same girl went into space, there would be less gravity acting upon her. Her body would become **weightless**, and she could float. She would still have the same mass (40 kilograms), but she would have very little or no weight.

On the moon you could kick a ball as far as the length of two football pitches. You could jump high enough to dunk a basketball with every jump. This all sounds great, but weightlessness also causes problems.

Astronauts and weightlessness

The human body, like other animals' bodies, is designed to deal with Earth's gravity. Without gravity, our bodies struggle to do the jobs they are supposed to do. Muscles become slack. Bones break more easily. When astronauts first went into space, NASA did not know this. Astronauts began to have serious health problems after being in space. NASA has developed exercises that astronauts must do while in space to keep their muscles active.

Weightlessness causes other problems for space travel besides slack muscles and brittle bones. Bread crumbs, salt, and pepper could cause a disaster if they floated into the air system. NASA food scientists had to develop liquid salt and pepper to prevent just such a problem. They give astronauts tortillas to eat in place of bread because tortillas do not "crumb" in the same way. Food, showering, even brushing teeth needed to be altered to allow for weightlessness.

Without gravity, human bodies have no weight.

Take a good look around your room. What would it look like if dirty laundry, books, paper, pens, shoes, CDs, and bed linens floated through the air? That is what would happen without gravity. Astronauts must be very neat and put tools, clothing, and books back in place. They must strap down anything they do not want floating around the space vehicle.

When a space flight finally reaches another planet, gravity and weight will be a new challenge. What would a 40-kilogram girl weigh on another planet? That depends on the planet. Other planets and the moon have different amounts of gravity, depending on their mass.

The moon's gravity is 0.17. What would you weigh on the moon?

Work it out

What would you weigh on the moon? The moon's gravity is 0.17. Work out your own mass in kilograms to find the answer!

Answers to "Work it out"

What is mass? (page 5)

Abby and Emma have a combined mass of 61 kilograms. Luke and Jamie have a combined mass of 62 kilograms. Those are the best pairings to come close to balancing.

What units are used when measuring mass? (page 15)

Add 300 + 80 + 7.63 to equal 387.63 grams.

What is weight? (page 19)

Convert 50 kilograms to 50,000 grams. 50,000 ÷ 125 = 400 bags.

What units Are used when measuring weight? (page 23)

The bananas weigh 1 pound 3 ounces.
1 pound = 454 grams.
1 ounce = 28 grams.
3 ounces x 28 = 84 grams.
454 grams + 84 grams = 538 grams.

What is weightlessness? (page 28)

Multiply your weight in kilograms by 0.17 to work out what your weight would be on the moon.

Glossary

acceleration to speed up or slow down

atom the smallest particle of something that can exist

balance tool for determining weight or mass

barleycorn grain of barley once used for measuring

carat unit for measuring the mass of gems

density mass per unit of volume

displace when an object takes the place of another. Displacement is used to determine an object's volume.

engineer person trained to design, build, or work with machines

estimate approximate judgement of size

force a push or pull

fulcrum support or point of rest for a beam in a balance

gravity universal force that acts between all objects

indicator pointer on a dial

kilogram metric mass equal to 1,000 grams or 2.2 pounds; measure of mass

mass measure of how much matter or "stuff" an object has

Newton basic unit of force

standard accepted as the model or authority

volume amount of space inside an object

weight measure of the pull of gravity on an object; it is a force equal to the mass of an object times the acceleration of gravity on that object and is measured in Newtons

weightless when an object (or person) has little or no weight

Find out more

Books

How Do We Measure?: Weight, Chris Woodward (Blackbirch Press, 2005)

Secret Treasures and Magical Measures: Adventures in Measuring: Time, Temperature, Length, Weight, Volume, Angles, Shapes, and Money, Chris Kensler (Kaplan Publishing, 2003)

Websites

Schoool.co.uk: Mass and weight
http://lgfl.skoool.co.uk/content/keystage3/Physics/pc/learningsteps/MWGLC/launch.html
Learn about the difference between mass and weight.

BBC skillswise
http://www.bbc.co.uk/skillswise/numbers/measuring/lwc/index.shtml
Use this website to make sure you understand about measuring weight.

BBC schools
http://www.bbc.co.uk/schools/ks2bitesize/maths/shape_space/measures/read1.shtml
Learn all about measurements on this website.

Reading scales
http://rwp.qia.oxi.net/learning_material/portal/measuring-weight_num_e3/m05/t02/index.htm
Practise reading scales on this web page.

Index